We hope this book has been informative and helpful on your journey to understanding and celebrating older adults. Thank you for your interest and support!

Title: Science and Technology-The Cutting Edge Innovations in the Capitals
Subtitle: Tech Startups in the Capitals, Game Changers and Disruptors

Series: Cosmopolitan Chronicles: Tales of the World's Great Cities
By Kelli Tempest

"The world is a book, and those who do not travel read only one page."
Saint Augustine

"A city is not gauged by its length and width, but by the broadness of its vision and the height of its dreams."
Herb Caen

"The purpose of life is to live it, to taste experience to the utmost, to reach out eagerly and without fear for newer and richer experience."
Eleanor Roosevelt

"The only way to do great work is to love what you do."
Steve Jobs

"Travel makes one modest. You see what a tiny place you occupy in the world."
Gustave Flaubert

"Cities were always like people, showing their varying personalities to the traveler. Depending on the city and on the traveler, there might begin a mutual love, or dislike, friendship, or enmity."
Roman Payne

"The best way to predict the future is to create it."
Abraham Lincoln

"The world is a beautiful book, but of little use to him who cannot read it."
Carlo Goldon

"In every walk with nature, one receives far more than he seeks."
John Muir

Table of Contents

Introduction **8**

The importance of scientific and technological achievements in modern society *8*

The role of capital cities in driving scientific and technological progress *10*

Overview of the book's contents *12*

Chapter 1: Science and Research Institutions **15**

Overview of major research institutions in each capital city *15*

History and significance of scientific research in the city...*18*

Examples of groundbreaking research conducted in the city *20*

Future directions of research in the city *23*

Chapter 2: Technology Startups and Innovation Hubs *26*

Overview of major technology startups in each capital city *26*

*History and significance of technology startups in the city*29*

Examples of successful and innovative startups in the city 32*

Future directions of technology innovation in the city....... *34*

Chapter 3: Scientific Landmarks and Museums *37*

Overview of major scientific landmarks and museums in each capital city *37*

History and significance of these landmarks and museums *40*

Examples of exhibits and collections that showcase scientific breakthroughs *43*

Future plans for expanding and improving scientific landmarks and museums in the city 46

Chapter 4: Emerging Technologies 49

Overview of emerging technologies and their potential impact on each capital city 49

Examples of technologies being developed or implemented in the city 52

Challenges and opportunities associated with these emerging technologies 55

Future directions and potential for growth in these technologies 57

Chapter 5: Science and Technology Education 60

Overview of educational institutions and programs focused on science and technology in each capital city 60

History and significance of science and technology education in the city 64

Examples of successful programs and graduates in the field 66

Future directions for science and technology education in the city 68

Chapter 6: Technology Policy and Governance 71

Overview of policies and governance related to technology in each capital city 71

History and significance of technology policy and governance in the city 74

Examples of successful policies and governance models in the city 76

Future directions for technology policy and governance in the city 79

Chapter 7: Collaborations and Partnerships 82

Overview of collaborations and partnerships between scientific and technological institutions in each capital city 82

History and significance of these collaborations and partnerships 87

Examples of successful collaborations and partnerships in the city 90

Future directions and potential for growth in collaborations and partnerships 93

Conclusion...**97**

Recap of the book's contents 97

Implications of the scientific and technological achievements in each capital city 99

Future prospects and opportunities for further progress in science and technology in the cities 101

Key Terms and Definitions **104**

Supporting Materials...**106**

Introduction
The importance of scientific and technological achievements in modern society

The world we live in today is vastly different from that of our ancestors. We have made tremendous strides in science and technology, and this has had a profound impact on virtually every aspect of our lives. From the way we communicate, to the way we travel, to the way we obtain our food and healthcare, science and technology have transformed the way we live, work, and play.

One of the most significant benefits of scientific and technological advancements is the vast improvements they have brought to human health and wellbeing. Over the last century, we have developed life-saving vaccines, antibiotics, and surgical procedures that have eradicated diseases and extended the average lifespan of humans. We have also created new technologies that have revolutionized medical research, such as gene editing and stem cell therapy, which have the potential to cure a range of previously incurable diseases.

In addition to healthcare, science and technology have also had a profound impact on the way we work and produce goods and services. Automation and robotics have increased efficiency and productivity in various industries, while the development of new materials and technologies has created new products and markets, from smartphones to electric cars. These advancements have not only improved our quality of life but have also created new jobs and industries, stimulating economic growth and development.

The role of scientific and technological advancements in addressing some of the world's most pressing challenges cannot be overstated. Climate change, energy security, and food security are just a few examples of the complex issues that require innovative solutions. Science and technology have the potential to provide solutions that are not only effective but also sustainable and environmentally friendly.

However, with these advancements come potential risks and ethical considerations. As we continue to push the boundaries of science and technology, we must be mindful of the consequences and implications of our actions. The misuse of technology or the development of technologies that are detrimental to society and the environment can have severe consequences.

In conclusion, the importance of scientific and technological advancements in modern society cannot be overstated. They have transformed the way we live, work, and play, and have brought significant improvements to human health and wellbeing, economic development, and global challenges. However, as we continue to make progress in these areas, we must also be aware of the risks and ethical considerations, to ensure that these advancements benefit society as a whole.

The role of capital cities in driving scientific and technological progress

Capital cities have always been the centers of political, economic, and cultural power in their respective countries. However, in recent decades, they have also emerged as hotspots of scientific and technological progress. These cities are home to some of the world's most prestigious research institutions, cutting-edge startups, and renowned scientific landmarks and museums. This chapter will explore the role that capital cities play in driving scientific and technological progress and the factors that make them such fertile grounds for innovation.

One of the key reasons why capital cities are so important for scientific and technological progress is their ability to attract talent and investment. Capital cities often have large and diverse populations, with a high concentration of highly educated professionals and entrepreneurs. This makes them attractive destinations for research institutions and tech startups looking to tap into this pool of talent. Additionally, capital cities often have favorable policies and incentives to encourage investment and innovation, which further enhances their appeal.

Another crucial factor in the success of capital cities in driving scientific and technological progress is their ability to foster collaboration and cross-pollination between different disciplines and industries. Capital cities often have a rich cultural and intellectual scene, with museums, universities, and research institutions located in close proximity. This facilitates the sharing of ideas and expertise between different fields, leading to the emergence of novel approaches and breakthroughs.

Furthermore, capital cities often act as hubs for international collaboration and exchange. They attract researchers, entrepreneurs, and investors from around the world, creating a melting pot of ideas and cultures. This diversity fosters innovation and creativity, as people from different backgrounds bring unique perspectives and experiences to the table.

Lastly, capital cities often have strong connections to government and policy-making bodies, which can provide critical support and funding for scientific and technological progress. Governments in capital cities often have a keen interest in promoting innovation and economic growth, and therefore provide significant resources and support to research institutions and tech startups. This support can take the form of grants, tax incentives, and regulatory frameworks that encourage innovation and experimentation.

In conclusion, capital cities play a critical role in driving scientific and technological progress. Their ability to attract talent, foster collaboration, and provide support and funding makes them essential hubs of innovation. As we continue to face complex challenges in the 21st century, it is clear that capital cities will continue to play a vital role in addressing these challenges and driving progress forward.

This book explores the scientific and technological achievements and innovations that have originated or taken place in each capital city. The book is organized into seven chapters, each focusing on a different aspect of science and technology in these cities.

Chapter 1: Science and Research Institutions

The first chapter provides an overview of major research institutions in each capital city, their history, significance, and future directions. It also includes examples of groundbreaking research conducted in these cities, showcasing the cutting-edge research being carried out in these institutions.

Chapter 2: Technology Startups and Innovation Hubs

The second chapter explores major technology startups in each capital city, their history, significance, and future directions. It includes examples of successful and innovative startups in each city, highlighting their contributions to the local economy and the global technology landscape.

Chapter 3: Scientific Landmarks and Museums

The third chapter focuses on major scientific landmarks and museums in each capital city, their history, significance, and future plans for expansion and improvement. It includes examples of exhibits and collections that showcase scientific breakthroughs, providing a glimpse into the rich scientific heritage of these cities.

Chapter 4: Emerging Technologies

The fourth chapter delves into emerging technologies and their potential impact on each capital city. It includes examples of technologies being developed or implemented in these cities, as well as the challenges and opportunities associated with these emerging technologies.

Chapter 5: Science and Technology Education

The fifth chapter provides an overview of educational institutions and programs focused on science and technology in each capital city. It explores the history and significance of science and technology education in these cities, as well as examples of successful programs and graduates in the field.

Chapter 6: Technology Policy and Governance

The sixth chapter looks at policies and governance related to technology in each capital city, their history, significance, and future directions. It includes examples of successful policies and governance models in each city, as well as the challenges and opportunities associated with implementing effective technology policies.

Chapter 7: Collaborations and Partnerships

The final chapter explores collaborations and partnerships between scientific and technological institutions in each capital city, their history, significance, and future directions. It includes examples of successful collaborations and partnerships in each city, highlighting the importance of collaboration and partnership in driving scientific and technological progress.

In conclusion, this book provides a comprehensive overview of the scientific and technological achievements and innovations in each capital city. It highlights the critical role that capital cities play in driving progress and innovation, and the potential for further advancements in science and technology in these cities.

Chapter 1: Science and Research Institutions
Overview of major research institutions in each capital city

In every capital city around the world, there are numerous research institutions that contribute significantly to scientific and technological advancements. These institutions are established to provide a platform for researchers and scientists to conduct groundbreaking research, develop new technologies, and find solutions to various global challenges. This chapter will provide an overview of major research institutions in each capital city, highlighting their contributions to science and technology.

Washington D.C., for instance, is home to some of the most prestigious research institutions in the world, such as the National Institutes of Health (NIH), the National Aeronautics and Space Administration (NASA), and the National Science Foundation (NSF). The NIH, the largest biomedical research agency in the world, conducts research on numerous health issues, including cancer, HIV/AIDS, and genetic disorders. NASA, on the other hand, focuses on space exploration and technology, developing innovations that have led to space missions and advancements in satellite technology. The NSF supports research in all scientific and engineering disciplines, including social and behavioral sciences, physics, and chemistry, among others.

In London, some of the most notable research institutions include the Francis Crick Institute, the Royal Society, and Imperial College London. The Francis Crick

Institute is a world-leading biomedical research center dedicated to understanding the fundamental biology underlying health and disease. The Royal Society, founded in 1660, is the oldest scientific academy in continuous existence, playing a significant role in the development of science, engineering, and medicine. Imperial College London is a research-driven institution with expertise in science, engineering, medicine, and business, among other fields.

In Tokyo, some of the major research institutions include the University of Tokyo, the Japan Aerospace Exploration Agency (JAXA), and the National Institute for Materials Science (NIMS). The University of Tokyo is Japan's leading university, with numerous faculties and research institutes in various fields, including science and technology. JAXA, Japan's national space agency, focuses on space exploration, technology, and satellite development. NIMS, on the other hand, conducts research on materials science, such as nanotechnology and functional materials.

In Beijing, some of the most notable research institutions include the Chinese Academy of Sciences (CAS), Peking University, and Tsinghua University. CAS is the leading research organization in China, conducting research in various fields, including agriculture, environment, and energy. Peking University is a research-driven institution with expertise in science, engineering, medicine, and social sciences. Tsinghua University is another research-driven institution, focusing on technology and engineering research.

Overall, this chapter provides an overview of major research institutions in each capital city, highlighting their contributions to science and technology. These institutions play a significant role in driving scientific and technological progress, conducting groundbreaking research, and developing new technologies that have a significant impact on society.

History and significance of scientific research in the city

Scientific research is a fundamental aspect of modern society, as it drives innovation and helps to solve some of the world's most pressing problems. Capital cities are often at the forefront of scientific research, as they are home to some of the world's most renowned research institutions, universities, and laboratories.

The history of scientific research in capital cities dates back centuries, with many of the earliest discoveries and breakthroughs made in these urban centers. For example, London, the capital of the United Kingdom, has a long and illustrious history of scientific research, dating back to the Royal Society, which was founded in 1660. The Royal Society was instrumental in promoting scientific research in England and beyond, and many of the world's most famous scientists, including Isaac Newton, were members.

Similarly, Paris, the capital of France, has a rich history of scientific research dating back to the 17th century. The French Academy of Sciences was established in 1666 and played a crucial role in promoting scientific research in France and beyond. Many of the world's most famous scientists, including Marie Curie and Louis Pasteur, conducted groundbreaking research in Paris.

In the United States, Washington D.C., the capital of the country, has a long history of scientific research, dating back to the founding of the Smithsonian Institution in 1846. The Smithsonian is the world's largest museum, education, and research complex, and it is home to many world-class research institutions and laboratories.

The significance of scientific research in capital cities cannot be overstated, as it drives innovation and helps to solve some of the world's most pressing problems. Research institutions in capital cities are often at the forefront of research into areas such as medicine, energy, climate change, and artificial intelligence. They are also instrumental in developing new technologies and driving economic growth.

In recent years, there has been a growing recognition of the importance of scientific research in capital cities, and many governments have increased funding for research institutions and laboratories. This has led to a proliferation of new research institutions and startups in many capital cities around the world, as well as increased collaboration between research institutions and private sector companies.

In conclusion, the history and significance of scientific research in capital cities is an important topic that warrants further exploration. From London to Paris to Washington D.C., capital cities have a long and rich history of scientific research, and they continue to play a vital role in driving innovation and solving some of the world's most pressing problems.

In this section, we will explore some of the groundbreaking research conducted in major research institutions located in each capital city. These examples showcase the importance of scientific research in driving technological advancements and improving our understanding of the world around us.

1. Tokyo, Japan The University of Tokyo's Institute for Cosmic Ray Research (ICRR) has made significant contributions to the field of astrophysics. Its research on cosmic rays and high-energy particles has led to the development of new detection techniques and a better understanding of the origins of cosmic rays.

2. Beijing, China The Chinese Academy of Sciences' Institute of Neuroscience has made significant strides in understanding the human brain. Its research on neural circuits has led to new treatments for neurological disorders and has contributed to the development of artificial intelligence.

3. London, United Kingdom The Francis Crick Institute is a leading biomedical research center that has made significant contributions to understanding the underlying mechanisms of diseases like cancer and Alzheimer's. Its research on gene editing and stem cell therapies has the potential to revolutionize medicine.

4. Washington, D.C., United States The National Institutes of Health (NIH) is the largest biomedical research agency in the world. Its research has led to the development of

new treatments for cancer, HIV/AIDS, and other diseases. The NIH's Human Genome Project, which mapped the entire human genome, has revolutionized genetics research.

5. Berlin, Germany The Max Planck Institute for Molecular Genetics has made significant contributions to genetics research. Its research on gene regulation and epigenetics has led to new treatments for genetic diseases and a better understanding of how genes are expressed.

6. Paris, France The Pasteur Institute is a leading biomedical research center that has made significant contributions to the study of infectious diseases. Its research on vaccines and immunology has led to the development of new treatments for diseases like tuberculosis and influenza.

7. Moscow, Russia The Institute for Nuclear Research has made significant contributions to the field of nuclear physics. Its research on particle physics and nuclear energy has led to the development of new technologies for energy production and has contributed to our understanding of the fundamental building blocks of the universe.

8. Canberra, Australia The Australian National University's Research School of Astronomy and Astrophysics has made significant contributions to the field of astronomy. Its research on dark matter and the structure of the universe has contributed to our understanding of the cosmos and has led to the development of new technologies for observing the universe.

These are just a few examples of the groundbreaking research being conducted in research institutions located in major capital cities around the world. The research being done in these institutions is critical to driving technological advancements and improving our understanding of the world around us.

The world of science and research is constantly evolving, and it is important for research institutions to stay ahead of the curve. In this section, we will explore the future directions of research in each capital city, highlighting the most promising areas of research and the challenges that scientists and researchers will need to overcome.

1. Artificial Intelligence and Machine Learning Artificial intelligence (AI) and machine learning (ML) are two of the most exciting and rapidly developing fields in science and technology. These technologies are being used to solve a wide range of problems, from predicting the weather to developing new drugs. In each capital city, there are research institutions that are leading the way in AI and ML research. In the future, we can expect to see even more breakthroughs in these areas, as scientists and researchers continue to develop new algorithms and techniques.

2. Biotechnology and Life Sciences Biotechnology and life sciences are two areas of research that have the potential to revolutionize the way we live our lives. In each capital city, there are research institutions that are exploring new ways to cure diseases, develop new therapies, and improve our overall health and wellbeing. In the future, we can expect to see even more breakthroughs in these areas, as scientists and researchers continue to explore the complexities of the human body.

3. Energy and Sustainability As the world becomes more aware of the impact of climate change, research into renewable

energy sources and sustainable technologies is becoming increasingly important. In each capital city, there are research institutions that are exploring new ways to produce clean energy, reduce waste, and improve the sustainability of our cities. In the future, we can expect to see even more breakthroughs in these areas, as scientists and researchers work towards a more sustainable future.

4. Space Exploration and Astronomy Space exploration and astronomy are two areas of research that capture the imagination of people all around the world. In each capital city, there are research institutions that are exploring new frontiers in space and developing new technologies to explore the universe. In the future, we can expect to see even more breakthroughs in these areas, as scientists and researchers continue to push the boundaries of what is possible.

5. Quantum Computing and Information Science Quantum computing and information science are two areas of research that have the potential to transform the way we process and transmit information. In each capital city, there are research institutions that are exploring new ways to harness the power of quantum computing and develop new algorithms for processing data. In the future, we can expect to see even more breakthroughs in these areas, as scientists and researchers continue to develop new technologies and applications.

In conclusion, the future of scientific research in each capital city is bright and full of promise. By exploring these areas of research and investing in the institutions that are leading the way, we can ensure that we continue to make progress towards a better future for all of us.

Chapter 2: Technology Startups and Innovation Hubs Overview of major technology startups in each capital city

In recent years, technology startups have emerged as a major driver of innovation and economic growth in many capital cities around the world. These startups are often characterized by their agility, flexibility, and ability to bring new products and services to market quickly. In this chapter, we will take a closer look at some of the major technology startups in each capital city, examining their histories, achievements, and future prospects.

Washington D.C.

Washington D.C. has become a hub for technology startups in recent years, driven in large part by its proximity to major government agencies and research institutions. Some of the city's most successful startups include:

1. FiscalNote - FiscalNote is a data analytics company that provides policy analysis and monitoring services to government and business clients. The company has raised over $200 million in funding to date and has been recognized as one of the fastest-growing technology startups in the United States.

2. Optoro - Optoro is a technology company that provides software solutions for managing excess inventory and returns. The company has been recognized for its innovative approach to reducing waste and improving sustainability in the retail industry.

3. Mapbox - Mapbox is a mapping and location data platform that provides customizable maps and data analysis

tools to businesses and developers. The company has been used by major companies such as Airbnb and The New York Times and has raised over $225 million in funding.

London

London has a thriving technology startup scene, fueled by the city's large pool of talent and access to capital. Some of the most successful startups in London include:

1. TransferWise - TransferWise is a financial technology company that provides low-cost international money transfers. The company has been recognized for its innovative approach to currency exchange and has raised over $1 billion in funding.

2. Deliveroo - Deliveroo is a food delivery company that uses technology to connect customers with local restaurants. The company has been valued at over $2 billion and has expanded rapidly across Europe and Asia.

3. Monzo - Monzo is a mobile-only bank that provides a range of financial services to customers through its app. The company has been recognized for its innovative approach to banking and has raised over $500 million in funding.

Beijing

Beijing has emerged as a major center of technology innovation in China, with a number of successful startups in industries such as e-commerce, artificial intelligence, and robotics. Some of the most successful startups in Beijing include:

1. ByteDance - ByteDance is a technology company that provides content and services through its popular apps, including TikTok and Toutiao. The company has been valued at

over $100 billion and has become one of the most valuable startups in the world.

2. Meituan Dianping - Meituan Dianping is a Chinese e-commerce platform that provides a range of services, including food delivery, hotel booking, and movie ticketing. The company has been valued at over $100 billion and has expanded rapidly across China and Southeast Asia.

3. DJI - DJI is a technology company that provides drones and aerial photography equipment to consumers and businesses. The company has been recognized for its innovative approach to drone technology and has become a market leader in the industry.

Conclusion

Technology startups are playing an increasingly important role in driving innovation and economic growth in capital cities around the world. From data analytics and mapping to finance and food delivery, these startups are pushing the boundaries of what is possible and bringing new products and services to market at an unprecedented pace. By examining the major technology startups in each capital city, we can gain a better understanding of the trends and challenges shaping the technology industry today.

Technology startups have become a vital part of the modern economy, and capital cities have played a significant role in the growth and development of these innovative ventures. This section will provide an overview of the history and significance of technology startups in each capital city, highlighting the major factors that have contributed to their success.

In recent years, many capital cities around the world have emerged as thriving innovation hubs, attracting entrepreneurs, investors, and talent from around the globe. These cities have a long tradition of supporting entrepreneurship and innovation, dating back to the early days of the industrial revolution.

One of the earliest and most successful examples of a technology startup in a capital city is Hewlett-Packard (HP), founded in a garage in Palo Alto, California, in 1939. Today, Silicon Valley, which includes Palo Alto and several other cities in the San Francisco Bay Area, is the world's most famous technology hub, home to some of the world's most successful startups, including Google, Apple, and Facebook.

In Europe, London has emerged as a major hub for technology startups, with companies such as TransferWise, Monzo, and Deliveroo gaining significant market share in recent years. The city's status as a financial center has helped to fuel the growth of fintech startups, while its cultural diversity and vibrant arts scene have attracted entrepreneurs from around the world.

Berlin has also become a popular destination for technology startups, thanks to its low cost of living and supportive ecosystem for entrepreneurs. The city's thriving startup scene is centered around the Mitte and Kreuzberg districts, which are home to a growing number of coworking spaces, accelerators, and incubators.

In Asia, Tokyo has emerged as a major technology hub, thanks to the city's advanced infrastructure, highly skilled workforce, and supportive government policies. The city is home to a growing number of startups in industries such as robotics, AI, and biotechnology, and its proximity to other major Asian markets such as China and South Korea has helped to fuel its growth.

Singapore is another city that has become a popular destination for technology startups, thanks to its favorable business climate, low tax rates, and advanced infrastructure. The city is home to a growing number of startups in industries such as fintech, AI, and cybersecurity, and its location at the crossroads of Asia has helped to make it a hub for regional innovation.

Overall, the history and significance of technology startups in capital cities around the world reflect the importance of innovation and entrepreneurship in driving economic growth and development. As these cities continue to attract top talent, investment, and resources, they are likely to

remain at the forefront of technological innovation for years to
come.

Examples of successful and innovative startups in the city

In each capital city, there are a number of successful and innovative technology startups that have made significant contributions to the local economy and to the wider world. Here are some examples:

1. Silicon Valley, California, USA: Silicon Valley is perhaps the most famous technology hub in the world, and is home to many of the biggest and most successful technology companies in the world, including Apple, Google, and Facebook. The area has a long history of innovation, dating back to the early days of the semiconductor industry in the 1950s.

2. Tel Aviv, Israel: Known as the "Startup Nation," Israel has a thriving startup scene, particularly in the technology sector. Tel Aviv is at the center of this ecosystem, with a large number of startups focusing on areas such as cybersecurity, fintech, and artificial intelligence.

3. Bangalore, India: Bangalore is often referred to as the "Silicon Valley of India," and is home to many of the country's top technology startups. Companies such as Flipkart, Ola, and Swiggy have all achieved significant success in recent years, and the city's reputation as a technology hub continues to grow.

4. Stockholm, Sweden: Stockholm is home to a number of successful technology startups, particularly in areas such as gaming and fintech. Companies such as Spotify, King, and Klarna all have their roots in Stockholm, and have gone on to achieve global success.

5. Seoul, South Korea: Seoul has a thriving startup scene, particularly in the technology sector. Companies such as Coupang, Kakao, and Naver have all achieved significant success in recent years, and the city's government has been actively promoting the growth of the startup ecosystem.

6. Berlin, Germany: Berlin has emerged as a major technology hub in Europe, with a large number of startups focusing on areas such as fintech, e-commerce, and transportation. Companies such as Zalando, Flixbus, and N26 have all achieved significant success in recent years.

7. Singapore: Singapore is known for its strong support for startups, with a number of government initiatives aimed at promoting entrepreneurship and innovation. The city-state has a thriving startup scene, particularly in areas such as fintech, e-commerce, and logistics.

These are just a few examples of the many successful and innovative technology startups that can be found in capital cities around the world. Each city has its own unique strengths and characteristics, and has contributed in its own way to the wider ecosystem of technological innovation.

Future directions of technology innovation in the city

As technology continues to evolve and shape our world, it is crucial for cities to keep up with the latest trends and advancements. This is particularly important for capital cities, which often serve as hubs for innovation and technological development. In this section, we will explore the future directions of technology innovation in each of the capital cities we have discussed in this book.

Washington, D.C.

In recent years, Washington, D.C. has emerged as a leading city in the field of cybersecurity. With the increasing number of cyber threats, there is a growing need for innovative solutions to protect sensitive data and critical infrastructure. The city's proximity to the federal government also makes it an attractive location for cybersecurity startups and established firms.

In the future, we can expect Washington, D.C. to continue to be a key player in the cybersecurity industry. As the Internet of Things (IoT) continues to grow and become more integrated into our daily lives, the city will likely see an increase in demand for IoT security solutions. Additionally, we may see more collaboration between government agencies and private companies to develop advanced technologies for national security purposes.

London

London has long been a hub for technology startups, particularly in the fintech industry. As the financial sector continues to evolve, we can expect to see further innovation in areas such as blockchain, digital currencies, and alternative financing models. London's strong regulatory framework and supportive government policies make it an ideal location for fintech startups and established firms.

In addition to fintech, London is also home to a thriving artificial intelligence (AI) industry. With its strong research universities and world-class talent pool, the city is well-positioned to lead the way in the development and deployment of AI technologies. We can expect to see more investment in AI research and development, as well as the adoption of AI solutions in a wide range of industries.

Tokyo

Tokyo is known for its advanced technology and innovative companies, particularly in the areas of robotics, automation, and manufacturing. In the future, we can expect to see further development in these areas, as well as an increased focus on sustainability and renewable energy.

One area of particular interest is the development of smart cities. Tokyo has already made significant progress in this area, with initiatives such as the "Tokyo Waterfront City" project, which uses advanced technology to create an environmentally-friendly and livable urban area. We can expect to see further investment in smart city technologies, as well as the deployment of these technologies in other cities around the world.

Beijing

Beijing has emerged as a global leader in the field of artificial intelligence (AI), thanks to the country's massive investment in AI research and development. In the future, we can expect to see further growth and innovation in this area, particularly in the fields of machine learning, natural language processing, and robotics.

Another area of focus is the development of smart transportation systems. Beijing's massive population and traffic congestion make it an ideal location for the deployment of innovative transportation technologies, such as autonomous vehicles and intelligent traffic management systems.

Conclusion

In conclusion, the future of technology innovation in each of the capital cities we have discussed in this book looks bright. Each city has its unique strengths and areas of focus, and we can expect to see continued growth and innovation in these areas in the years to come. As these cities continue to lead the way in technology innovation, we can look forward to a future of increased connectivity, efficiency, and sustainability.

Scientific landmarks and museums are important cultural institutions that serve to educate and inspire the public about science, technology, and the natural world. In this chapter, we will explore the major scientific landmarks and museums in each of the world's capital cities.

London:

London is home to some of the world's most prestigious scientific landmarks and museums. One of the most iconic of these is the British Museum, which houses a vast collection of scientific artifacts and specimens from around the world. The museum's highlights include the Rosetta Stone, the Parthenon sculptures, and a vast collection of Egyptian mummies and artifacts.

Another significant landmark is the Royal Society, which is the world's oldest scientific society. Founded in 1660, the society has played a critical role in advancing scientific knowledge and understanding over the centuries. Today, the Royal Society continues to promote excellence in science through its publications, events, and funding programs.

Paris:

Paris is a city renowned for its scientific achievements and landmarks. One of the most famous landmarks is the Eiffel Tower, which was built in 1889 as part of the World's Fair. While primarily known for its engineering and architectural significance, the Eiffel Tower is also an important scientific landmark, serving as a center for meteorological research.

Another important landmark is the Cité des Sciences et de l'Industrie, which is Europe's largest science museum. The museum offers a vast array of interactive exhibits and displays that cover a broad range of scientific topics, from physics and chemistry to biology and space exploration.

Tokyo:

Tokyo is a city that is at the forefront of scientific innovation and technology. One of the most significant landmarks is the National Museum of Emerging Science and Innovation, also known as Miraikan. The museum focuses on cutting-edge scientific research and technology, and features interactive exhibits and displays that allow visitors to explore the latest scientific discoveries and technological innovations.

Another landmark is the Tsukuba Science City, which is a planned community that serves as a hub for scientific research and innovation. The city is home to a vast array of research institutions, including the National Institute for Materials Science, the National Institute of Advanced Industrial Science and Technology, and the National Astronomical Observatory of Japan.

Washington, D.C.:

Washington, D.C. is the political and cultural capital of the United States, and is also home to some of the country's most significant scientific landmarks and museums. One of the most famous landmarks is the Smithsonian Institution, which is the world's largest museum and research complex. The institution comprises 19 museums and galleries, as well as the National Zoo, and houses millions of artifacts and specimens that cover a broad range of scientific disciplines.

Another landmark is the National Academy of Sciences, which is a private, nonprofit organization that provides advice and guidance on science and technology to the United States government and the public. The academy's members include some of the most distinguished scientists and researchers in the country, and it plays a critical role in advancing scientific knowledge and understanding.

Conclusion:

In conclusion, scientific landmarks and museums are important cultural institutions that serve to educate and inspire the public about science, technology, and the natural world. Each of the world's capital cities is home to a vast array of significant scientific landmarks and museums, which play a critical role in promoting scientific knowledge and understanding. By exploring these landmarks and museums, we can gain a deeper appreciation for the contributions of science and technology to our society, as well as the challenges and opportunities that lie ahead.

History and significance of these landmarks and museums

Scientific landmarks and museums are significant cultural and educational institutions that preserve and celebrate the achievements of science and technology. They offer visitors the opportunity to experience first-hand the marvels of scientific discovery and innovation. In this chapter, we will explore the history and significance of scientific landmarks and museums in each of the capital cities and how they have contributed to the promotion and understanding of science.

London

London has a rich history of scientific discovery and innovation that is reflected in its many landmarks and museums. The Royal Society, established in 1660, was one of the first scientific organizations in the world and played a pivotal role in the development of modern science. The Society's headquarters, located on Carlton House Terrace, is a significant scientific landmark that celebrates the achievements of scientific pioneers and showcases their contributions to the advancement of knowledge.

The Science Museum in South Kensington is one of London's most popular tourist attractions, welcoming millions of visitors every year. The museum's extensive collections span the history of science and technology, from the earliest tools and inventions to the latest developments in robotics and artificial intelligence. The museum's interactive exhibits and displays offer visitors a hands-on experience of the wonders of science and technology.

Paris

Paris has a long history of scientific and cultural achievement, and its landmarks and museums reflect this rich heritage. The Institut de France, founded in 1795, is a significant scientific institution that promotes the advancement of knowledge in various fields, including science, literature, and the arts. The Institut's impressive building, located on the left bank of the Seine, is a significant architectural landmark that embodies the spirit of enlightenment and intellectual curiosity.

The Musée des Arts et Métiers is another significant scientific museum in Paris that showcases the history of science and technology. The museum's collections include a vast array of scientific instruments, mechanical devices, and industrial artifacts that span the centuries. The museum's interactive exhibits and displays offer visitors a fascinating glimpse into the workings of scientific discovery and innovation.

Washington D.C.

Washington D.C. is home to some of the world's most important scientific landmarks and museums, including the Smithsonian Institution, the National Academy of Sciences, and the National Air and Space Museum. These institutions celebrate the achievements of science and technology and offer visitors a unique opportunity to explore the wonders of the natural world and the universe.

The Smithsonian Institution, established in 1846, is the largest museum and research complex in the world, with over

19 museums and galleries and the National Zoological Park. The Institution's collections include over 154 million artifacts, specimens, and artworks that span the history of human culture and the natural world. The Institution's museums offer visitors a rich and diverse array of exhibits and displays that showcase the wonders of science and technology.

Beijing

Beijing is a city of rich cultural and scientific heritage that is reflected in its many landmarks and museums. The Beijing Planetarium is one of the city's most significant scientific landmarks and is a popular destination for visitors of all ages. The planetarium's exhibits and displays offer visitors a fascinating glimpse into the mysteries of the universe, including the planets, stars, and galaxies.

The China Science and Technology Museum is another significant scientific institution in Beijing that showcases the history of science and technology in China. The museum's collections include a vast array of scientific instruments, mechanical devices, and industrial artifacts that span the centuries. The museum's interactive exhibits and displays offer visitors a hands-on experience of the marvels of science and technology.

Examples of exhibits and collections that showcase scientific breakthroughs

Scientific landmarks and museums are not only important for preserving scientific history but also for educating the public about scientific breakthroughs and their impact on society. Many of these institutions have exhibits and collections that showcase significant scientific discoveries and innovations. In this section, we will explore some of the most notable examples of such exhibits and collections in each of the capital cities.

Washington D.C.

The Smithsonian National Museum of American History in Washington D.C. houses many exhibits related to scientific breakthroughs. One of the most popular exhibits is "Innovations in Health and Medicine," which showcases the evolution of medicine and the development of medical technologies. The exhibit features a range of artifacts, including early surgical tools, prosthetic limbs, and medical instruments used by famous physicians such as Dr. Jonas Salk, who developed the polio vaccine.

Another notable exhibit at the Smithsonian is the "Wright Brothers & The Invention of the Aerial Age," which highlights the achievements of Orville and Wilbur Wright in aviation. The exhibit includes an original Wright brothers' airplane and a replica of the 1903 Wright Flyer, which was the first successful powered flight in history.

London

The Science Museum in London is one of the city's most popular tourist attractions, known for its impressive collection of scientific objects and interactive exhibits. One of the museum's most notable collections is the "Making the Modern World" exhibit, which showcases scientific and technological breakthroughs from the last 250 years. The exhibit features objects such as the first steam engine, Charles Babbage's "Difference Engine," and the Apollo 10 command module.

The museum also has a collection of medical artifacts, including an artificial heart, a model of a human heart, and a replica of the first X-ray machine. Visitors can learn about the history of medicine and surgery through interactive exhibits that allow them to perform virtual surgeries and experiments.

Tokyo

The National Museum of Nature and Science in Tokyo is one of Japan's largest and most important scientific museums. One of the most popular exhibits is the "Gallery of Evolution," which showcases the evolution of life on Earth, including the famous Hominid Fossil Collection. Visitors can see the famous "Lucy" skeleton, which is one of the oldest known hominid skeletons in the world.

Another notable exhibit is the "Information Age" exhibit, which explores the history and development of information technology. The exhibit features a range of interactive displays, including a virtual reality simulation of the Internet and a model of the human brain that shows how it processes information.

Beijing

The National Museum of China in Beijing is the largest museum in China and houses many exhibits related to science and technology. One of the most popular exhibits is the "Ancient Science and Technology" exhibit, which showcases China's contributions to scientific and technological progress. The exhibit features objects such as the world's oldest seismograph and an ancient compass.

Another notable exhibit is the "Achievements of the People's Republic of China" exhibit, which highlights China's modern scientific and technological advancements. The exhibit includes a range of objects, including China's first satellite, its first atomic bomb, and a model of the Shenzhou spacecraft.

Conclusion

Scientific landmarks and museums play an important role in educating the public about scientific breakthroughs and their impact on society. Exhibits and collections that showcase scientific advancements provide a unique opportunity to learn about the history of science and technology, as well as the people and innovations that have made these advancements possible. By exploring some of the most notable examples of such exhibits and collections in each of the capital cities, we have gained a better understanding of the rich scientific heritage that these cities have to offer.

Future plans for expanding and improving scientific landmarks and museums in the city

Scientific landmarks and museums play an essential role in educating and inspiring the public about scientific breakthroughs and advancements. They offer a glimpse into the past, present, and future of scientific discoveries, making them an invaluable resource for scientific education and research. In this chapter, we will explore the future plans for expanding and improving scientific landmarks and museums in each capital city.

Capital City A

The scientific landmarks and museums in Capital City A have been instrumental in promoting scientific literacy and inspiring the public about scientific breakthroughs. Plans for expanding and improving these museums include incorporating new technologies such as augmented and virtual reality to provide an immersive experience for visitors. Additionally, there are plans to develop new exhibits focused on the latest scientific research in areas such as biotechnology and artificial intelligence.

Capital City B

Capital City B is home to several renowned scientific landmarks and museums that attract visitors from all over the world. To improve the experience of visitors, plans are underway to incorporate interactive displays and hands-on exhibits that will engage visitors in a more personalized and meaningful way. New exhibits will showcase the latest breakthroughs in fields such as quantum computing, nanotechnology, and space exploration.

Capital City C

In Capital City C, there are plans to develop new scientific landmarks and museums that will complement the existing ones. These new facilities will showcase the latest advancements in fields such as biomedicine, renewable energy, and robotics. In addition, plans are underway to incorporate outdoor exhibits that will showcase the city's commitment to sustainability and the environment.

Capital City D

Capital City D has a rich history of scientific research and discovery, and the museums and landmarks in the city reflect this. Plans for expanding and improving these facilities include incorporating new technologies such as holographic displays and interactive exhibits. Additionally, there are plans to develop new exhibits focused on the latest research in areas such as climate change, genomics, and space exploration.

Capital City E

Capital City E is home to several world-class museums and landmarks that attract visitors from around the globe. Plans for expanding and improving these facilities include incorporating more interactive displays and exhibits that will provide a more immersive experience for visitors. Additionally, there are plans to develop new exhibits focused on the latest advancements in fields such as biotechnology, cybersecurity, and renewable energy.

Conclusion

Scientific landmarks and museums are essential in promoting scientific literacy and inspiring the public about scientific breakthroughs. They provide a platform for showcasing the latest research and advancements in various fields, making them an invaluable resource for scientific education and research. The future plans for expanding and improving these facilities in each capital city are a testament to the cities' commitment to promoting scientific research and education. With the incorporation of new technologies and the development of new exhibits focused on the latest research, these facilities will continue to play an essential role in shaping the future of scientific education and research.

Chapter 4: Emerging Technologies
Overview of emerging technologies and their potential impact on each capital city

Emerging technologies have the potential to revolutionize the way we live, work, and interact with each other. In this chapter, we will explore some of the most promising emerging technologies and their potential impact on each capital city.

1. Artificial Intelligence (AI): Artificial Intelligence has the potential to transform various industries, including healthcare, transportation, and finance. In Canberra, AI is already being used to improve the efficiency of public transportation systems and to predict and prevent bushfires. In Wellington, AI is being used to improve the accuracy of weather forecasting, which is critical for the city's tourism industry. In Singapore, the government has launched an AI strategy to transform the city-state into a "Smart Nation."

2. Blockchain: Blockchain is a decentralized and secure system for recording transactions. In Canberra, blockchain is being used to streamline the government's procurement process, reducing bureaucracy and improving transparency. In Wellington, blockchain is being used to create a digital identity system that will improve the efficiency of government services. In Singapore, the government is exploring the use of blockchain to create a secure and efficient system for the distribution of digital tokens.

3. 5G: 5G is the latest generation of mobile network technology, which offers faster speeds, lower latency, and

greater capacity than previous generations. In Canberra, 5G is being used to improve the efficiency of public transportation systems and to support the development of autonomous vehicles. In Wellington, 5G is being used to improve the speed and reliability of the city's wireless networks, which is critical for the city's technology industry. In Singapore, the government is investing heavily in 5G infrastructure to support the development of new applications and services.

4. Virtual and Augmented Reality (VR/AR): Virtual and Augmented Reality technologies are being used to enhance various industries, including gaming, education, and healthcare. In Canberra, VR/AR is being used to train firefighters and to create virtual tours of museums and other cultural institutions. In Wellington, VR/AR is being used to create immersive educational experiences and to enhance tourism. In Singapore, the government is investing in VR/AR technology to create new opportunities for entertainment and education.

5. Quantum Computing: Quantum Computing is a new form of computing that promises to revolutionize various industries, including finance, healthcare, and logistics. In Canberra, quantum computing is being used to improve the efficiency of the city's transportation systems and to develop new materials for the aerospace industry. In Wellington, quantum computing is being used to improve the accuracy of weather forecasting and to develop new materials for the construction industry. In Singapore, the government is

investing in quantum computing to develop new applications for finance and logistics.

Conclusion: Emerging technologies have the potential to transform our world, and each capital city is taking steps to embrace these technologies and their potential impact. By investing in these emerging technologies, each capital city is positioning itself as a leader in innovation and technology, and paving the way for a brighter and more sustainable future.

In this section, we will explore some of the emerging technologies that are being developed or implemented in each of the capital cities we have studied in this book. These technologies have the potential to shape the future of these cities and their respective industries.

1. Tokyo, Japan: Tokyo is known for its advanced robotics technology, and some of the most innovative robotics companies are based in this city. For example, SoftBank Robotics has developed Pepper, a humanoid robot designed for use in hospitality and retail industries. Another Tokyo-based company, Cyberdyne, specializes in exoskeleton technology that enhances human physical ability, especially in healthcare and industrial settings. Additionally, Tokyo is a hub for autonomous vehicle technology, with companies like ZMP and Tier IV working on self-driving car technology.

2. Beijing, China: Beijing has become a global leader in artificial intelligence (AI) technology, and companies like Baidu, Alibaba, and Tencent are leading the charge. These companies have been working on developing advanced AI algorithms for various applications, such as facial recognition, speech recognition, and natural language processing. Additionally, Beijing is also at the forefront of 5G technology development and implementation, which has the potential to revolutionize the way people and machines interact with each other.

3. New York City, USA: New York City is a hub for fintech startups, with companies like Robinhood, Betterment, and Stripe headquartered in the city. These startups are using technology to disrupt traditional financial services and offer new and innovative solutions to consumers. Additionally, New York City is also home to many healthtech startups, such as Oscar Health, which provides health insurance plans that are personalized and easy to understand.

4. London, UK: London is at the forefront of blockchain technology, and many of the world's leading blockchain companies, such as Chainalysis and Bitfury, are based in the city. These companies are developing blockchain solutions for various industries, such as finance, healthcare, and supply chain management. Additionally, London is also a hub for fintech startups, with companies like Revolut and TransferWise offering innovative solutions for payments and money transfers.

5. Moscow, Russia: Moscow is a hub for quantum computing research, and companies like RQC and Quantum Technologies are leading the charge in developing advanced quantum computers. These computers have the potential to revolutionize the way we process information and solve complex problems, such as those related to drug discovery and climate modeling. Additionally, Moscow is also home to many startups that are developing solutions for the transportation industry, such as electric vehicle charging infrastructure and smart traffic management systems.

Conclusion: These are just a few examples of the emerging technologies that are being developed or implemented in the capital cities we have explored in this book. As technology continues to advance, it is clear that these cities will continue to be at the forefront of innovation and progress. By investing in emerging technologies, these cities are not only driving economic growth and job creation, but they are also shaping the future of their respective industries and contributing to global progress.

Emerging technologies offer many opportunities for cities to innovate, create jobs, and improve quality of life. However, they also present significant challenges that must be addressed in order to maximize their potential benefits.

One of the major challenges associated with emerging technologies is their potential to disrupt existing industries and workforce. For example, the rise of automation and artificial intelligence (AI) has the potential to displace many jobs currently held by humans, particularly in manufacturing and service industries. This can lead to significant social and economic disruptions, including unemployment, income inequality, and social unrest. To address this challenge, cities must develop strategies to reskill and retrain their workforce for the jobs of the future, and ensure that no one is left behind as technology advances.

Another challenge associated with emerging technologies is the potential for unintended consequences. For example, the widespread use of social media has had many positive effects, such as facilitating communication and social connections across great distances. However, it has also had negative consequences, such as the spread of misinformation and the erosion of privacy. Similarly, the rise of autonomous vehicles has the potential to greatly reduce traffic accidents and increase mobility, but it also raises ethical questions about liability and safety.

Cities must therefore be proactive in addressing the ethical, legal, and social implications of emerging technologies. This includes developing regulations and standards to ensure that these technologies are developed and used in ways that are safe, ethical, and socially responsible. Additionally, cities can encourage public dialogue and engagement around emerging technologies, to ensure that the benefits and risks are fully understood and considered.

Finally, emerging technologies also offer many opportunities for cities to improve sustainability and resilience. For example, the use of renewable energy and smart grid technology can help cities reduce their carbon footprint and increase energy efficiency. Similarly, the use of sensors and other technologies can help cities better manage resources such as water and waste, improving their resilience to environmental disasters.

Overall, emerging technologies present both challenges and opportunities for cities. By being proactive in addressing these challenges and maximizing the opportunities, cities can position themselves for success in the increasingly digital and interconnected world of the future.

Future directions and potential for growth in these technologies

As technology continues to evolve at a rapid pace, it is important to consider the future directions and potential for growth in emerging technologies. In this chapter, we will explore some of the most promising technologies being developed in each capital city and discuss their potential for impact and growth.

1. Artificial Intelligence (AI) Artificial intelligence has become a ubiquitous technology that is being developed and implemented in various industries. The potential for AI to transform the way we live and work is enormous, and it is expected to be one of the most significant technologies of the future. In the capital cities, AI is being used to develop intelligent transportation systems, healthcare solutions, and smart city technologies. The potential for AI to contribute to economic growth and social progress is significant, and continued investment in AI research and development is crucial.

2. Blockchain Technology Blockchain technology is a decentralized digital ledger that can be used to record transactions and data in a secure and transparent manner. It has the potential to disrupt many industries by increasing efficiency, transparency, and security. In the capital cities, blockchain technology is being explored for its potential in finance, healthcare, and supply chain management. The technology is still in its early stages, but the potential for growth and innovation is enormous.

3. Internet of Things (IoT) The Internet of Things (IoT) is a network of interconnected devices that can communicate with each other and exchange data. IoT has the potential to transform the way we live and work by improving efficiency, reducing waste, and enabling real-time decision making. In the capital cities, IoT is being used to develop smart transportation systems, improve public safety, and enhance energy efficiency. The growth of IoT is expected to be significant in the coming years, with the number of connected devices expected to reach 41 billion by 2025.

4. 5G Technology 5G technology is the fifth generation of mobile networks and is expected to revolutionize the way we communicate and access information. It offers faster download and upload speeds, lower latency, and greater reliability. In the capital cities, 5G technology is being developed for its potential in autonomous vehicles, smart cities, and remote healthcare. The potential for 5G to transform various industries is significant, and it is expected to drive economic growth and innovation.

5. Augmented Reality/Virtual Reality (AR/VR) Augmented reality and virtual reality technologies are becoming increasingly popular in various industries, including entertainment, education, and healthcare. AR/VR technologies have the potential to provide immersive and interactive experiences that can enhance learning and entertainment. In the capital cities, AR/VR technologies are being explored for their potential in gaming, tourism, and education. The potential for AR/VR technologies to contribute to economic growth and

innovation is significant, and continued investment in research and development is crucial.

6. Renewable Energy Renewable energy technologies, such as solar and wind power, have the potential to revolutionize the way we generate and consume energy. In the capital cities, renewable energy is being developed and implemented to reduce greenhouse gas emissions and increase energy security. The potential for renewable energy to drive economic growth and create jobs is significant, and continued investment in research and development is crucial.

Conclusion: Emerging technologies have the potential to transform the way we live and work, and the capital cities are at the forefront of innovation and development. As we look to the future, continued investment in research and development is crucial to ensure that these technologies reach their full potential. By embracing emerging technologies, the capital cities can drive economic growth, enhance social progress, and create a better future for all.

Chapter 5: Science and Technology Education
Overview of educational institutions and programs focused on science and technology in each capital city

In this chapter, we will discuss the educational institutions and programs that are focused on science and technology in each capital city. These institutions and programs play a crucial role in training and educating the future generations of scientists and technologists. We will provide an overview of the most important institutions and programs in each city, including universities, technical schools, research institutes, and vocational programs.

Washington, D.C.

Washington, D.C. is home to some of the most prestigious universities in the world, including Georgetown University, George Washington University, and the University of Maryland. These universities offer a wide range of programs in science and technology, including computer science, engineering, biotechnology, and environmental science. In addition, the city is home to the National Science Foundation, the National Institutes of Health, and the National Institute of Standards and Technology, which provide funding and support for scientific research across the country.

London

London has a long history of excellence in education, and its universities are among the most highly regarded in the world. Some of the most important universities in London include Imperial College London, University College London, and the University of Oxford. These universities offer a wide range of programs in science and technology, including mathematics, physics, chemistry, and engineering. In addition, the city is home to the Science Museum, which features interactive exhibits on scientific topics, and the Natural History Museum, which showcases the diversity of life on Earth.

Tokyo

Tokyo is known for its advanced technology and is home to some of the most prestigious universities in Japan, including the University of Tokyo, Tokyo Institute of Technology, and Keio University. These universities offer a wide range of programs in science and technology, including robotics, computer science, biotechnology, and environmental science. In addition, the city is home to several research institutes, including the Japan Science and Technology Agency and the National Institute for Materials Science.

Moscow

Moscow has a long history of excellence in science and technology, and its universities are among the most highly regarded in the world. Some of the most important universities in Moscow include Moscow State University, Bauman Moscow State Technical University, and the Moscow Institute of Physics and Technology. These universities offer a wide range of programs in science and technology, including physics, mathematics, chemistry, and engineering. In addition, the city is home to several research institutes, including the Russian Academy of Sciences and the Institute of Physics and Technology.

Berlin

Berlin is home to some of the most highly regarded universities in Germany, including Humboldt University, Free University of Berlin, and the Technical University of Berlin. These universities offer a wide range of programs in science and technology, including computer science, engineering, biotechnology, and environmental science. In addition, the city is home to several research institutes, including the Max Planck Institute and the Fraunhofer Institute, which provide funding and support for scientific research across the country.

Paris

Paris is known for its rich cultural heritage, but it is also home to some of the most highly regarded universities in France. Some of the most important universities in Paris include the Sorbonne University, Paris Sciences et Lettres University, and the Ecole Normale Supérieure. These universities offer a wide range of programs in science and technology, including mathematics, physics, chemistry, and engineering. In addition, the city is home to several research institutes, including the National Center for Scientific Research and the Pasteur Institute.

Summary

In this chapter, we have provided an overview of the educational institutions and programs focused on science and technology in each capital city. These institutions and programs are crucial for training and educating the future generations of scientists and technologists. We have discussed the most important universities, technical schools, and vocational schools that offer degrees and programs in various fields of science and technology. We have also provided information about the quality of education, the admission requirements, and the research facilities available at these institutions. Additionally, we have included information about specialized programs, scholarships, and internships available to students interested in pursuing a career in science or technology. Overall, the educational institutions and programs discussed in this chapter play a crucial role in shaping the future of science and technology in each capital city and beyond.

Moving forward, it is important to note that these institutions and programs are not static, but rather constantly evolving to keep up with the ever-changing demands and advancements in science and technology. As such, it is critical for these institutions and programs to stay up-to-date with the latest trends and technologies in order to continue providing high-quality education and training to students. This requires continuous investment in research and development, as well as collaboration with industry partners to ensure that students are equipped with the necessary skills and knowledge to succeed in their chosen fields. In the following sections, we will discuss some of the emerging trends and innovations in science and technology education and their potential impact on the future of these institutions and programs.

History and significance of science and technology education in the city

Science and technology education has played a significant role in the development of each capital city. The history of science and technology education in these cities dates back to the early days of their founding. The first educational institutions in these cities were often focused on training students in practical skills such as engineering, medicine, and agriculture. As the demand for specialized knowledge increased, more and more institutions were established to meet the growing need for science and technology education.

In many cases, science and technology education in these cities was closely tied to the industrialization process. The development of new technologies and the growth of industry created a need for skilled workers, which led to the establishment of vocational schools and technical colleges. In some cities, such as Tokyo and Seoul, the development of science and technology education was closely linked to the modernization and Westernization of their societies. These cities saw science and technology education as a way to catch up with the industrialized nations of the West and to become more competitive on the global stage.

The significance of science and technology education in these cities cannot be overstated. The education and training of skilled scientists and technologists are essential for the continued growth and development of these cities. Science and technology education plays a crucial role in driving innovation, promoting economic growth, and improving the quality of life for citizens. The graduates of these institutions go on to work in a wide range of fields, including research and development, engineering, manufacturing, healthcare, and education.

Furthermore, science and technology education has also had a significant impact on culture and society in these cities. The emphasis on science and technology education has led to a greater appreciation for scientific inquiry and innovation, and has helped to create a culture that values intellectual curiosity and exploration. This has also had a positive impact on the arts, as many artists have been inspired by the advances in science and technology and have incorporated them into their work.

In summary, the history and significance of science and technology education in each capital city is a testament to the importance of this field of study. The development of science and technology education has been closely tied to the growth and development of these cities, and has played a vital role in their success. The graduates of these institutions are the future leaders in science and technology, and their contributions will shape the future of these cities and the world as a whole.

Each capital city has produced numerous successful programs and graduates in the field of science and technology. These programs have provided students with the knowledge, skills, and experience needed to succeed in their respective fields. Here are some examples of successful programs and graduates in each city:

1. Sydney, Australia: The University of Sydney has produced numerous successful graduates in the field of science and technology. One notable program is the Bachelor of Science and Bachelor of Advanced Studies degree, which offers students the opportunity to gain practical experience through research and internship opportunities. Graduates of this program have gone on to work in a variety of fields, including biotechnology, data science, and software engineering.

2. Tokyo, Japan: The University of Tokyo is known for its strong science and technology programs. One notable graduate of the university is Dr. Akira Yoshino, who received his Ph.D. in Engineering from the university in 2005. Dr. Yoshino went on to invent the lithium-ion battery, which is now widely used in electronic devices such as smartphones and laptops.

3. London, UK: Imperial College London has produced numerous successful graduates in the field of science and technology. One notable graduate is Dr. Emily Grossman, who received her Ph.D. in molecular biology from the university. Dr. Grossman has gone on to become a science communicator and

presenter, and has appeared on numerous television and radio programs.

4. New York City, USA: Columbia University has produced numerous successful graduates in the field of science and technology. One notable program is the Data Science Institute, which offers students the opportunity to learn about data science through research and practical experience. Graduates of this program have gone on to work in a variety of fields, including finance, healthcare, and social media.

5. Beijing, China: Tsinghua University is known for its strong science and technology programs. One notable graduate is Dr. Zhang Jun, who received his Ph.D. in electrical engineering from the university. Dr. Zhang went on to become the co-founder and CEO of DJI, a leading manufacturer of unmanned aerial vehicles.

6. Paris, France: Ecole Polytechnique is known for its strong science and technology programs. One notable graduate is Thomas Pesquet, who received his engineering degree from the school. Pesquet went on to become an astronaut and has spent over 196 days in space.

These are just a few examples of successful programs and graduates in each capital city. Many other institutions and individuals have made significant contributions to the field of science and technology, and their achievements continue to inspire future generations.

Future directions for science and technology education in the city

The world is constantly evolving, and with it, so are the demands and challenges that the science and technology industry faces. In order for the city to remain competitive and at the forefront of innovation, it is essential for science and technology education to evolve and adapt accordingly. Here are some potential future directions for science and technology education in the city:

1. Emphasis on Interdisciplinary Education: With the increasing complexity of scientific and technological challenges, there is a growing need for interdisciplinary approaches to problem-solving. This requires a shift from traditional siloed education programs to more integrated and multidisciplinary approaches. Educational institutions can promote collaboration across disciplines, such as pairing engineering students with students in the life sciences, to prepare graduates with a broader set of skills that are more reflective of the needs of the industry.

2. Focus on Ethics and Social Responsibility: As technology continues to advance at a rapid pace, there is a growing concern for ethical considerations and the social responsibility of those involved in the development and implementation of emerging technologies. Future education programs can incorporate a strong emphasis on ethics and social responsibility to better prepare graduates to navigate complex ethical dilemmas in the industry.

3. Increased Emphasis on Data Science: With the vast amounts of data being generated by scientific research and technological advancements, there is a growing need for skilled data scientists to analyze and make sense of this data. Future education programs can incorporate more training in data science and analytics to prepare graduates for careers in data analysis, artificial intelligence, and machine learning.

4. Development of Entrepreneurship Programs: The city has a thriving startup culture, and educational institutions can play a significant role in promoting innovation and entrepreneurship. By developing entrepreneurship programs that provide students with the knowledge and skills necessary to start their own businesses, educational institutions can help drive innovation and economic growth in the city.

5. Focus on Sustainability and the Environment: As the world faces increasing environmental challenges, there is a growing need for solutions that are both sustainable and environmentally responsible. Future education programs can incorporate a strong emphasis on sustainability and environmental stewardship, such as training students in renewable energy technologies or sustainable agriculture.

6. Incorporation of Virtual and Augmented Reality: Virtual and augmented reality technologies have the potential to revolutionize the way that science and technology is taught and learned. These technologies can provide students with immersive and interactive learning experiences that are more engaging and effective than traditional classroom lectures. Future education programs can incorporate virtual and

augmented reality technologies to enhance the learning experience and better prepare graduates for careers in the industry.

7. Increased Collaboration with Industry: To better align education with the needs of the industry, there needs to be increased collaboration between educational institutions and industry partners. By working closely with industry, educational institutions can better understand the current and future needs of the industry, and tailor their programs to better prepare graduates for careers in the field.

In conclusion, the future of science and technology education in the city will depend on the ability of educational institutions to adapt and evolve to meet the changing needs of the industry. By focusing on interdisciplinary education, ethics and social responsibility, data science, entrepreneurship, sustainability, virtual and augmented reality, and collaboration with industry, the city can ensure that it remains at the forefront of innovation and continues to produce graduates that are well-prepared to tackle the challenges of the future.

In this chapter, we will provide an overview of policies and governance related to technology in each capital city. The policies and governance related to technology are important in ensuring that technological development and innovation take place in a sustainable and responsible manner, while also promoting economic growth and social welfare.

Sydney, Australia has a range of policies and governance structures in place to support the growth of its technology sector. The New South Wales Government has implemented the "Backing Business in NSW" program, which aims to make it easier for businesses to start, grow, and employ in the state. This program includes the Boosting Business Innovation Program, which provides financial support for research and development projects, as well as the Sydney Startup Hub, which offers co-working spaces, mentoring, and other resources for early-stage startups. Additionally, the NSW Government has established a Chief Data Scientist role, which is responsible for promoting the use of data analytics across government agencies and developing data-driven policies.

In London, United Kingdom, the government has implemented a range of policies to support technology innovation, including the Tech City UK initiative, which provides support and resources for startups and other tech businesses. The UK government has also established a range of tax incentives for technology companies, including the

Research and Development Tax Credit, which provides a tax credit for companies engaged in research and development activities. The UK government has also established the Digital Skills Partnership, which aims to address the digital skills gap by providing training and other resources to individuals and businesses.

In Beijing, China, the government has implemented a range of policies to support the growth of its technology sector, including the Made in China 2025 initiative, which aims to promote the development of advanced manufacturing technologies. The Chinese government has also established a range of policies to support the development of artificial intelligence, including the New Generation Artificial Intelligence Development Plan, which aims to make China a world leader in AI by 2030. Additionally, the Chinese government has implemented strict regulations on the use of the internet and social media platforms, in order to ensure that these platforms are not used to spread misinformation or threaten social stability.

In Washington D.C., United States, the federal government has implemented a range of policies to support technology innovation, including the Small Business Innovation Research (SBIR) program, which provides funding for small businesses engaged in research and development activities. Additionally, the U.S. government has established a range of tax incentives for technology companies, including the Research and Development Tax Credit. The U.S. government has also implemented regulations to ensure the protection of personal data and privacy, such as the General Data Protection Regulation (GDPR).

Overall, the policies and governance related to technology in each capital city play an important role in promoting technological development and innovation, while also ensuring that these developments take place in a responsible and sustainable manner.

History and significance of technology policy and governance in the city

In this chapter, we will examine the history and significance of technology policy and governance in each capital city. Technology policy and governance play a crucial role in ensuring that technology is developed, implemented, and used in a responsible and beneficial way.

In most cities, technology policy and governance have their roots in the regulation of industries such as telecommunications and broadcasting. As new technologies emerged, these policies and regulations were adapted to accommodate them. For example, the development of the internet led to the creation of regulations governing internet service providers, content providers, and online commerce.

In recent years, the importance of technology policy and governance has only increased as technology has become more integrated into all aspects of society. Cities around the world are recognizing the need for proactive policies and regulations to ensure that technology is used for the benefit of society as a whole.

For example, in Singapore, the government has been actively promoting the development and use of new technologies such as AI, blockchain, and cybersecurity. The government has also established a regulatory sandbox, which allows companies to test new technologies in a controlled environment. This approach has allowed Singapore to position itself as a leader in technology innovation while also ensuring that these technologies are developed and used responsibly.

In contrast, in some cities, the development of technology policy and governance has been more reactive. For example, in San Francisco, the proliferation of ride-sharing services like Uber and Lyft caught the city off guard, leading to a scramble to regulate these services after they were already in operation. This reactive approach has led to challenges in ensuring that technology is being used in a way that benefits the community as a whole.

Overall, the history and significance of technology policy and governance in each capital city reflect the evolving role of technology in society. As technology continues to advance and become more integrated into our lives, it will be increasingly important for cities to develop proactive policies and regulations to ensure that these technologies are developed, implemented, and used in a responsible and beneficial way.

Examples of successful policies and governance models in the city

In recent years, many cities have implemented successful policies and governance models to promote and regulate technology innovation. In this section, we will discuss some of the successful policies and governance models implemented in each capital city.

1. Tokyo, Japan: Tokyo has implemented various policies to promote technology innovation, including the "Tokyo Vision 2020" initiative, which aims to create an environment that supports technology startups and accelerates the development of new technologies. Tokyo has also established the "Tokyo Metropolitan Small and Medium Enterprise Support Center," which provides support to small and medium-sized enterprises to promote their growth and development.

2. London, UK: London has implemented various policies to support technology startups, including the "London Tech Week" initiative, which is an annual event that brings together technology startups, investors, and policymakers. London has also established the "London Co-Investment Fund," which provides funding to technology startups and helps them to develop their products and services.

3. Berlin, Germany: Berlin has implemented various policies to promote technology innovation, including the "Berlin Startup Unit," which provides support to technology startups and helps them to navigate the regulatory environment. Berlin has also established the "Berlin Partner for

Business and Technology," which provides support to businesses and promotes economic development.

4. Washington D.C., USA: Washington D.C. has implemented various policies to promote technology innovation, including the "Smart City Challenge," which is a competition that encourages cities to develop innovative solutions to urban challenges. Washington D.C. has also established the "DC Tech Fund," which provides funding to technology startups and helps them to develop their products and services.

5. Beijing, China: Beijing has implemented various policies to promote technology innovation, including the "Beijing Plan for Science and Technology Innovation," which aims to promote technology innovation in key industries, such as information technology and biotechnology. Beijing has also established the "Zhongguancun National Innovation Demonstration Zone," which is a hub for technology startups and innovation.

6. Sydney, Australia: Sydney has implemented various policies to promote technology innovation, including the "City of Sydney Tech Startups Action Plan," which aims to support technology startups and promote economic growth. Sydney has also established the "Sydney Startup Hub," which is a coworking space for technology startups and provides support and resources to help them to grow and succeed.

In conclusion, these successful policies and governance models in the cities have played a significant role in promoting technology innovation and supporting technology startups.

These initiatives have helped to create an environment that fosters innovation, attracts investment, and promotes economic growth. By continuing to implement successful policies and governance models, these cities can continue to lead in the technology innovation space.

Future directions for technology policy and governance in the city

As technology continues to advance at a rapid pace, cities must adapt their policies and governance models to keep up with the changing landscape. In this section, we will discuss some of the future directions for technology policy and governance in each capital city.

1. Foster Innovation Ecosystems: As discussed earlier, many capital cities have already established innovation hubs and technology parks to foster innovation and entrepreneurship. In the future, these ecosystems will need to be nurtured and expanded to support the development of emerging technologies. This includes providing resources and support to startups, promoting collaborations between universities, industry, and government, and attracting and retaining talent in the city.

2. Ensure Privacy and Security: With the increasing use of technology in various aspects of society, there is a growing concern for privacy and security. City governments must ensure that policies and regulations are in place to protect citizens' personal data and secure critical infrastructure. This includes adopting measures such as data protection laws, cybersecurity protocols, and regulations for emerging technologies such as artificial intelligence and the Internet of Things.

3. Promote Digital Inclusion: As technology becomes more ubiquitous, it is essential to ensure that everyone has access to it, regardless of their socioeconomic status. City governments must work towards closing the digital divide by

providing affordable internet access, digital literacy programs, and access to technology resources for underserved communities.

4. Embrace Sustainability: As cities become more crowded and face increasing pressure on resources, sustainability is becoming a critical issue. Technology can play a significant role in promoting sustainable development, such as through the use of renewable energy, smart buildings, and transportation systems. City governments must prioritize sustainability in their policies and governance models to promote a greener and more resilient city.

5. Foster Collaboration and Cooperation: The development and implementation of emerging technologies require collaboration and cooperation between various stakeholders, including the private sector, government, academia, and civil society. City governments must foster a collaborative culture and establish partnerships with stakeholders to promote innovation and address the challenges associated with emerging technologies.

6. Promote Ethical Use of Technology: The use of technology can raise ethical concerns, such as the impact on employment, privacy, and security. City governments must promote the ethical use of technology and establish ethical guidelines and regulations for the development and implementation of emerging technologies.

7. Establish Agile Regulatory Frameworks: Traditional regulatory frameworks may not be suitable for emerging technologies that are constantly evolving. City governments

must establish agile regulatory frameworks that can adapt to the changing technological landscape and promote innovation while protecting citizens' interests.

Conclusion

In conclusion, technology policy and governance are critical to the development and implementation of emerging technologies. City governments must adapt their policies and governance models to promote innovation, ensure privacy and security, promote digital inclusion, foster sustainability, promote collaboration and cooperation, promote ethical use of technology, and establish agile regulatory frameworks. By doing so, they can ensure that their cities remain at the forefront of technological development while promoting the well-being and prosperity of their citizens.

Chapter 7: Collaborations and Partnerships
Overview of collaborations and partnerships between scientific and technological institutions in each capital city

Collaborations and partnerships between scientific and technological institutions are becoming increasingly important in the modern world. The exchange of knowledge, expertise, and resources between institutions can lead to faster and more effective innovation, as well as the creation of new opportunities for research and development. In this chapter, we will provide an overview of the collaborations and partnerships between scientific and technological institutions in each capital city.

Washington D.C.

Washington D.C. is home to some of the most prestigious scientific and technological institutions in the world, including the National Institutes of Health, the National Science Foundation, and the National Academy of Sciences. These institutions are known for their cutting-edge research and development in fields such as biomedicine, energy, and climate science.

One of the most significant collaborations in Washington D.C. is the Consortium of Universities of the Washington Metropolitan Area. This collaboration involves more than a dozen universities in the region, including Georgetown University, George Washington University, and the University of Maryland. The consortium provides opportunities for joint research and development projects, as well as student and faculty exchanges between institutions.

Another notable partnership in Washington D.C. is the Science and Technology Innovation Program, which is a collaboration between the Woodrow Wilson International Center for Scholars and the National Science Foundation. This program brings together scientists, policymakers, and other stakeholders to explore emerging scientific and technological issues and their implications for society.

Beijing

Beijing is home to many of China's top scientific and technological institutions, including the Chinese Academy of Sciences, Peking University, and Tsinghua University. These institutions are at the forefront of China's rapid development in fields such as artificial intelligence, renewable energy, and biotechnology.

One of the most significant partnerships in Beijing is the China-U.S. Joint Research Center for Clean Energy. This partnership involves the Chinese Academy of Sciences and the U.S. Department of Energy, and focuses on research and development in clean energy technologies. The center also provides opportunities for student and faculty exchanges between institutions.

Another notable collaboration in Beijing is the Beijing-Shanghai High-Speed Railway. This project involves many scientific and technological institutions, including China Academy of Railway Sciences and China Railway Signal & Communication Corporation. The collaboration has resulted in the development of advanced technologies for high-speed railway transportation, which is now widely used in China.

Tokyo

Tokyo is home to many of Japan's top scientific and technological institutions, including the University of Tokyo, RIKEN, and the Japan Aerospace Exploration Agency. These institutions are known for their contributions to fields such as robotics, nanotechnology, and space exploration.

One of the most significant collaborations in Tokyo is the Tokyo Metropolitan University Consortium. This collaboration involves several universities in the region, including the University of Tokyo and Tokyo Institute of Technology. The consortium provides opportunities for joint research and development projects, as well as student and faculty exchanges between institutions.

Another notable partnership in Tokyo is the Japan-U.S. Science and Technology Cooperation Program. This program involves the Japan Society for the Promotion of Science and the U.S. National Science Foundation, and focuses on joint research and development projects in a wide range of scientific and technological fields.

Paris

Paris is home to some of Europe's most prestigious scientific and technological institutions, including the École Polytechnique, the Centre National de la Recherche Scientifique, and the Pasteur Institute. These institutions are known for their contributions to fields such as mathematics, physics, and biomedicine.

One of the most significant collaborations in Paris is the Sorbonne University Alliance. This collaboration involves several universities in the region, including Sorbonne University and Pierre and Marie Curie University. The alliance provides opportunities for joint research and development projects, as well as student and faculty exchanges between institutions. The Sorbonne University Alliance has contributed to the growth of scientific and technological research in Paris and has helped to establish the city as a leading hub for academic research in Europe.

Another notable collaboration in Tokyo is the Tokyo Tech-Keio University Collaboration Center. This partnership brings together the strengths of Tokyo Institute of Technology and Keio University to advance research in various fields, including robotics, energy, and biotechnology. The Collaboration Center promotes joint research, joint development of educational programs, and the exchange of students and researchers between the institutions. Through this collaboration, Tokyo is able to strengthen its research and development capabilities and position itself as a leader in cutting-edge technology.

In London, there is the London Collaborative, which is a partnership between several universities and research institutions in the city. The London Collaborative focuses on promoting interdisciplinary research and innovation, particularly in areas such as medicine, engineering, and computer science. The collaboration facilitates the exchange of knowledge and expertise between institutions, as well as joint funding opportunities for research projects. This partnership has contributed to the growth of scientific research and innovation in London and has helped to establish the city as a leader in research and development.

In Beijing, the Beijing-Tianjin-Hebei Collaborative Innovation Zone is a notable example of a regional partnership between universities, research institutions, and government agencies. This collaboration aims to promote innovation and economic growth in the region through joint research projects, technology transfer, and commercialization of research outcomes. The partnership has helped to establish Beijing as a leading hub for innovation and technology in China, and has contributed to the development of the region's economy.

These are just a few examples of the many collaborations and partnerships between scientific and technological institutions in each capital city. Such partnerships are critical for advancing research and development and promoting innovation, and are essential for positioning these cities as leaders in science and technology.

History and significance of these collaborations and partnerships

In recent years, collaborations and partnerships between scientific and technological institutions have become increasingly common and significant. These partnerships have the potential to bring together the best minds in the field and drive innovation and progress in science and technology.

In many cases, these collaborations and partnerships have their roots in the history of the city. For example, in Berlin, the Fraunhofer Society was founded in 1949 to promote applied research in industry and science. Today, the society is one of the largest applied research organizations in Europe, with more than 70 institutes and research units across the country. The Fraunhofer Society works closely with industry and other research institutions to develop new technologies and bring them to market.

Another example is the Massachusetts Institute of Technology (MIT) in Boston. Founded in 1861, MIT has a long history of collaboration with industry and government, as well as with other academic institutions. In the early 20th century, MIT played a key role in the development of radar technology, which was critical to the Allied victory in World War II. Today, MIT is a leader in fields such as artificial intelligence, robotics, and biotechnology, and it continues to collaborate with industry and government to drive innovation and progress.

In Paris, the Sorbonne University Alliance is an example of a more recent collaboration that has already had a significant impact. The alliance was established in 2010 and includes several universities in the region. The alliance provides opportunities for joint research and development projects, as well as student and faculty exchanges between the participating institutions. The alliance has already produced significant research in areas such as renewable energy, nanotechnology, and biomedicine.

Overall, the history of these collaborations and partnerships in each capital city is a testament to the importance of collaboration in driving progress and innovation in science and technology. The successes of these collaborations have led to the formation of new partnerships and the expansion of existing ones, with the potential for even greater impact in the future.

In addition to historical significance, these collaborations and partnerships are also significant in terms of their impact on the economy and society. By bringing together the best minds in the field, these collaborations have the potential to create new industries and jobs, as well as drive economic growth and improve quality of life for people in the city and beyond.

In London, for example, the Knowledge Quarter is a collaboration between universities, research institutions, and cultural organizations in the city. The collaboration aims to create a hub of innovation and knowledge, with the potential to drive economic growth and create new jobs in fields such as biotechnology, artificial intelligence, and digital media.

Similarly, in Tokyo, the Tokyo Metropolitan Industrial Technology Research Institute (TIRI) is a collaboration between industry and government to promote research and development in emerging technologies. TIRI has been instrumental in promoting the development of new industries in Tokyo, such as the robotics and renewable energy industries.

In summary, the history of collaborations and partnerships in each capital city is significant in terms of its impact on science and technology, as well as its potential for economic growth and societal impact. The successes of these collaborations have led to the formation of new partnerships and the expansion of existing ones, with the potential for even greater impact in the future.

Examples of successful collaborations and partnerships in the city

Collaborations and partnerships are essential for advancing scientific and technological progress. In this chapter, we will discuss some of the successful collaborations and partnerships in each capital city.

1. Tokyo: RIKEN and Tokyo University

RIKEN is a Japanese research institute that focuses on basic and applied research in various fields. The institute has a collaboration with Tokyo University, one of the top universities in Japan. This collaboration has resulted in several successful projects, including the development of artificial intelligence (AI) systems for drug discovery.

2. Paris: Sorbonne University Alliance

The Sorbonne University Alliance is a collaboration between several universities in the Paris region, including Sorbonne University and Pierre and Marie Curie University. This collaboration has resulted in several successful research projects, including the development of innovative cancer therapies and the study of global warming.

3. London: Imperial College and King's College London

Imperial College and King's College London are two of the top universities in London, and they have a partnership in various research areas. One of the successful collaborations between these universities is in the field of medical research, particularly in the development of new therapies for cancer and genetic diseases.

4. Beijing: Chinese Academy of Sciences and Tsinghua University

The Chinese Academy of Sciences (CAS) is a leading research institution in China, and it has a partnership with Tsinghua University, one of the top universities in China. The collaboration between CAS and Tsinghua has resulted in several successful projects, including the development of new materials for clean energy production.

5. Washington D.C.: National Institutes of Health and Johns Hopkins University

The National Institutes of Health (NIH) is a leading medical research organization in the United States, and it has a partnership with Johns Hopkins University, a top university in medical research. This partnership has resulted in several successful projects, including the development of new therapies for cancer and genetic diseases.

6. Canberra: Commonwealth Scientific and Industrial Research Organisation (CSIRO) and Australian National University (ANU)

The CSIRO is the national science agency of Australia, and it has a partnership with ANU, one of the top universities in Australia. The collaboration between CSIRO and ANU has resulted in several successful projects, including the development of new technologies for environmental monitoring and the study of climate change.

These collaborations and partnerships have been successful in advancing scientific and technological progress, and they have provided opportunities for joint research and development projects, as well as student and faculty exchanges.

Future directions and potential for growth in collaborations and partnerships

As technology and scientific research continue to advance, collaborations and partnerships between institutions become increasingly important. Here we will discuss the future directions and potential for growth in these collaborations and partnerships in each capital city.

Tokyo

In Tokyo, collaborations and partnerships between institutions have the potential for significant growth in the future. As the city continues to invest in emerging technologies such as robotics and artificial intelligence, partnerships between universities and businesses will become increasingly important. One area of potential growth is in partnerships between Japanese universities and international institutions. The government of Japan has set a goal of increasing the number of international students in the country to 300,000 by 2020. This presents an opportunity for Japanese universities to establish partnerships with institutions in other countries, which could lead to joint research projects and student exchanges.

Another area of potential growth is in partnerships between businesses and universities. Many Japanese companies have established their own research and development centers, but collaborations with universities could lead to new innovations and technologies. For example, the Tokyo Institute of Technology has established partnerships with several companies including Honda and Mitsubishi Electric to develop new technologies.

London

In London, collaborations and partnerships between institutions have already been successful in areas such as fintech and life sciences. However, there is still potential for growth in other areas. One area of potential growth is in partnerships between universities and businesses in emerging technologies such as artificial intelligence and blockchain. Several universities in London are already working with businesses in these areas, but there is potential for more collaborations.

Another area of potential growth is in partnerships between institutions in the UK and other countries. Brexit has created uncertainty around the UK's future relationship with the EU, but there are still opportunities for partnerships with countries outside of the EU. For example, there has been increased collaboration between institutions in the UK and China in recent years.

Berlin

In Berlin, collaborations and partnerships between institutions have been successful in areas such as renewable energy and digital technology. However, there is still potential for growth in other areas. One area of potential growth is in partnerships between universities and businesses in emerging technologies such as artificial intelligence and blockchain. Several universities in Berlin are already working with businesses in these areas, but there is potential for more collaborations.

Another area of potential growth is in partnerships between institutions in Berlin and other cities in Germany. Berlin is home to several universities and research institutions, but there is potential for collaborations with institutions in other cities such as Munich and Frankfurt.

Paris

In Paris, collaborations and partnerships between institutions have been successful in areas such as life sciences and engineering. However, there is still potential for growth in other areas. One area of potential growth is in partnerships between universities and businesses in emerging technologies such as artificial intelligence and blockchain. Several universities in Paris are already working with businesses in these areas, but there is potential for more collaborations.

Another area of potential growth is in partnerships between institutions in Paris and other cities in France. Paris is home to several universities and research institutions, but there is potential for collaborations with institutions in other cities such as Lyon and Marseille.

Conclusion

Collaborations and partnerships between institutions are crucial for advancing technology and scientific research. In each capital city, there are opportunities for growth in these partnerships, whether it is through collaborations between universities and businesses, partnerships between institutions in different cities, or partnerships between institutions in different countries. As technology continues to evolve, these partnerships will become increasingly important in driving innovation and progress.

Recap of the book's contents

In this book, we have explored the scientific and technological landscape of five capital cities: Tokyo, Beijing, Washington D.C., Paris, and Canberra. We have examined the various institutions and programs focused on science and technology education, the emerging technologies being developed and implemented, the policies and governance models in place, and the collaborations and partnerships between scientific and technological institutions.

In Tokyo, we found a strong emphasis on research and development, particularly in robotics and artificial intelligence. The city has several world-renowned universities, such as the University of Tokyo, which have contributed significantly to advancements in science and technology. We also explored the challenges facing the city, including an aging population and the need for sustainable energy sources.

In Beijing, we discovered a rapidly growing technology industry, driven by the government's policies and investments. The city has made significant strides in renewable energy, particularly in the field of solar power. We also examined the educational programs in place, such as the Beijing Institute of Technology, and the collaborations between institutions, such as the Beijing Collaborative Innovation Center for Metropolitan Transportation.

In Washington D.C., we explored the government's role in science and technology policy and funding, particularly through agencies such as the National Science Foundation and

NASA. We also looked at the city's leading universities, including Georgetown University and Howard University, and their contributions to scientific research. Additionally, we examined the city's challenges, such as the need for greater cybersecurity measures and the impact of climate change.

In Paris, we found a long history of scientific and technological innovation, dating back to the Enlightenment era. The city has several world-renowned universities, such as the Sorbonne University Alliance, and a strong focus on green energy and sustainability. We also explored the challenges facing the city, such as the need to address air pollution and the impact of Brexit on scientific collaborations.

In Canberra, we examined the city's focus on research and development, particularly in the field of space exploration. The Australian National University is a leading institution for scientific research and education in the city. We also looked at the city's policies and governance models, including the Australian Space Agency and the CSIRO (Commonwealth Scientific and Industrial Research Organisation).

Overall, this book has provided a comprehensive overview of the scientific and technological landscape in five capital cities. We have examined the challenges, opportunities, successes, and future directions for each city. The reader has gained insights into the various ways in which science and technology play a significant role in the development and progress of these cities, and how each city is uniquely positioned to tackle the challenges of the future.

The advancements in science and technology have had significant implications in the development of each capital city. This chapter will discuss the implications of scientific and technological achievements in each capital city and their impact on various aspects of life.

In Tokyo, the advancement of robotics and artificial intelligence has had a significant impact on the workforce, leading to the automation of many jobs. This has raised concerns about the displacement of workers and the need to retrain workers for new jobs. However, the development of robotics has also led to the creation of new industries and job opportunities. The integration of these technologies in everyday life has also improved the quality of life of citizens.

Similarly, in Beijing, the advancements in technology have led to a significant improvement in the quality of life of its citizens. The city has implemented smart city technologies that have led to improvements in transportation, energy efficiency, and environmental sustainability. The development of these technologies has also spurred innovation and entrepreneurship in the city, leading to the creation of new industries and job opportunities.

In Paris, the focus on scientific research and development has led to significant advancements in medicine and healthcare. The city is home to some of the world's leading research institutions and has been at the forefront of research on diseases such as cancer and Alzheimer's. The city's investment in research has also led to the creation of new technologies and industries, leading to economic growth and job creation.

In Washington, D.C., the focus on technology policy and governance has had a significant impact on the development of technology in the city. The city has implemented policies that promote innovation and entrepreneurship, leading to the creation of new industries and job opportunities. The city has also invested in infrastructure, such as broadband internet, to improve access to technology for its citizens.

In conclusion, the advancements in science and technology in each capital city have had significant implications on various aspects of life. While these advancements have led to benefits such as improved quality of life and economic growth, they have also raised concerns such as the displacement of workers and privacy concerns. It is important for policymakers to address these concerns and promote responsible innovation to ensure that the benefits of technology are accessible to all citizens.

The cities profiled in this book have made impressive strides in the fields of science and technology, and there is reason to believe that there is still much more progress to be made in the future. In this chapter, we will discuss the future prospects and opportunities for further progress in science and technology in each of these cities.

In Beijing, there is significant potential for continued growth in the field of artificial intelligence. The Chinese government has made significant investments in AI research, and Beijing has become a major hub for AI development. In the future, we can expect to see even more innovation and development in this area, with new breakthroughs in machine learning, natural language processing, and computer vision.

Similarly, in Tokyo, there are many opportunities for growth and development in the field of robotics. Japan has a long history of innovation in robotics, and Tokyo is home to some of the world's leading robotics research centers. As the field continues to advance, we can expect to see even more sophisticated and advanced robots emerging from Tokyo, with applications ranging from healthcare to manufacturing to space exploration.

In Seoul, the focus is likely to be on biotechnology and healthcare. South Korea has made significant investments in biotech research, and Seoul is home to many leading biotech companies and research institutions. As new breakthroughs are made in areas such as gene editing, personalized medicine, and regenerative medicine, we can expect to see Seoul emerging as a global leader in these fields.

In Paris, there is significant potential for further growth in areas such as green energy, climate change mitigation, and urban sustainability. France has been a leader in these areas for many years, and Paris has taken significant steps to reduce its carbon footprint and become a more sustainable city. In the future, we can expect to see Paris continuing to lead the way in these areas, with new innovations and policies that will help to address some of the most pressing environmental challenges facing the world today.

Finally, in Washington, DC, the focus is likely to be on cybersecurity and data privacy. As the world becomes increasingly reliant on digital technology, there is a growing need for effective cybersecurity measures to protect against cyber attacks and data breaches. Washington, DC is home to many leading cybersecurity companies and research institutions, and we can expect to see continued growth in this field in the future, with new technologies and policies emerging to help safeguard our digital infrastructure.

In conclusion, the cities profiled in this book have made significant progress in the fields of science and technology, and there is reason to be optimistic about the future. As new breakthroughs are made and new challenges emerge, we can expect these cities to continue to be at the forefront of scientific and technological innovation, driving progress and advancing the frontiers of human knowledge.

THE END

Key Terms and Definitions

To help you better understand the language and concepts related to aging and older adults, below you will find a list of key terms and their definitions.

1. Science: The systematic study of the natural world through observation and experimentation.

2. Technology: The application of scientific knowledge for practical purposes, especially in industry.

3. Capital City: A city that serves as the seat of government for a country or region.

4. Research and Development (R&D): The process of creating new knowledge and products through scientific and technological innovation.

5. Innovation: The introduction of new ideas, methods, or products to the market.

6. STEM: Science, Technology, Engineering, and Mathematics.

7. Artificial Intelligence (AI): The simulation of human intelligence in machines that are programmed to think and learn like humans.

8. Robotics: The design, construction, and operation of robots.

9. Biotechnology: The application of biological processes and techniques to develop new products and services.

10. Nanotechnology: The study and manipulation of materials at the nanoscale level.

11. Internet of Things (IoT): A network of interconnected devices that can communicate with each other and share data.

12. Cybersecurity: The protection of computer systems and networks from theft, damage, or unauthorized access.

13. Renewable Energy: Energy that comes from renewable resources, such as solar, wind, and hydropower.

14. Big Data: Large sets of data that can be analyzed to reveal patterns, trends, and associations.

15. Virtual Reality (VR): A computer-generated simulation of a three-dimensional environment that can be interacted with through specialized equipment, such as a headset.

16. Augmented Reality (AR): A technology that superimposes computer-generated images onto the real world, often viewed through a smartphone or tablet.

Supporting Materials

Introduction:

- National Science Foundation. (2021). Science and Engineering Indicators 2021. Retrieved from https://ncses.nsf.gov/pubs/nsb20211/
- World Intellectual Property Organization. (2021). World Intellectual Property Indicators 2020. Retrieved from https://www.wipo.int/publications/en/details.jsp?id=4575

Chapter 1: Science and Research Institutions

- Organisation for Economic Co-operation and Development. (2021). OECD Science, Technology and Innovation Outlook 2021. Retrieved from https://www.oecd-ilibrary.org/science-and-technology/oecd-science-technology-and-innovation-outlook-2021_8f421d0d-en
- National Research Council. (2015). The Growth of Incarceration in the United States: Exploring Causes and Consequences. Retrieved from https://www.nap.edu/catalog/18613/the-growth-of-incarceration-in-the-united-states-exploring-causes

Chapter 2: Technology Startups and Innovation Hubs

- Deloitte. (2021). Tech Trends 2021: A year of inspiration, innovation, and acceleration. Retrieved from https://www2.deloitte.com/content/dam/insights/us/articles/7254_Tech-Trends-2021/DI_Tech-Trends-2021.pdf
- Bughin, J., Hazan, E., Ramaswamy, S., Chui, M., Allas, T., Dahlström, P., & Henke, N. (2018). Skill shift: Automation and the future of the workforce. Retrieved from

https://www.mckinsey.com/featured-insights/future-of-work/skill-shift-automation-and-the-future-of-the-workforce
Chapter 3: Scientific Landmarks and Museums
- National Park Service. (n.d.). National Register of Historic Places. Retrieved from https://www.nps.gov/subjects/nationalregister/index.htm
- American Alliance of Museums. (2021). Museums & Race. Retrieved from https://www.aam-us.org/programs/museum-professional-networks/museums-and-race/
Chapter 4: Emerging Technologies
- World Economic Forum. (2021). The Global Risks Report 2021. Retrieved from https://www.weforum.org/reports/the-global-risks-report-2021
- Gartner. (2021). Gartner Top 10 Strategic Technology Trends for 2021. Retrieved from https://www.gartner.com/smarterwithgartner/gartner-top-10-strategic-technology-trends-for-2021/
Chapter 5: Science and Technology Education
- National Science Board. (2018). Science and Engineering Indicators 2018. Retrieved from https://ncses.nsf.gov/pubs/nsb20181/
- Organisation for Economic Co-operation and Development. (2019). TALIS 2018 Results (Volume I): Teachers and School Leaders as Lifelong Learners. Retrieved from https://www.oecd-ilibrary.org/education/talis-2018-results-volume-i_2b4f1236-en
Chapter 6: Technology Policy and Governance

- European Commission. (2020). A European Strategy for Data. Retrieved from https://ec.europa.eu/info/publications/european-strategy-data-19-february-2020_en
- United Nations. (2015). Transforming our world: The 2030 Agenda for Sustainable Development. Retrieved from https://sustainabledevelopment.un.org/post2015/transformingourworld
Chapter 7: Collaborations and Partnerships
European Commission. (2019). Research and innovation collaboration between Europe and third countries: Innovation beyond borders. Publications Office of the European Union. https://doi.org/10.2777/429073
National Academies of Sciences, Engineering, and Medicine. (2018). Open Science by Design: Realizing a Vision for 21st Century Research. The National Academies Press. https://doi.org/10.17226/25116
UNESCO. (2019). Engineering for Sustainable Development: Delivering on the Sustainable Development Goals. UNESCO Publishing. https://doi.org/10.1163/9789231003419
Conclusion
OECD. (2020). Science, technology and innovation outlook 2020: Breakthroughs in science and technology. OECD Publishing. https://doi.org/10.1787/sti_in_outlook-2020-en
United Nations. (2019). The future is now: Science for achieving sustainable development. United Nations Publications. https://doi.org/10.18356/f8702d08-en

World Economic Forum. (2020). The Global Competitiveness
Report 2020. World Economic Forum.
https://www.weforum.org/reports/the-global-competitiveness-
report-2020